# JOHNNIE WALKER'S

## BIOGRAPHY

The Inspiring Journey of a
Legendary DJ his Impact
Music and Broadcasting.

**ECHO's OF THE AIRWAVES**

**Andrew Manny**

# DISCLAIMER

The following book is meant only for reading enjoyment and information. There is no commitment or guarantee of any kind attached to the information provided. Although every effort has been made to present correct and up-to-date information, it is entirely the reader's obligation to verify any material before relying on it.

Any mistakes or omissions cannot be attributed to the publisher or author. The author or publisher shall not be subject to any legal liability or blame for any compensation, damages, or financial loss resulting from the information provided, whether in direct or indirect relation.

Images and trademarks are used without authorization. The trademark owners do not approve of, support, or link use of the trademark. All trademarks and images featured in this book are used solely for clarification and have not been utilized with the intention of violating their owners.

## DEDICATION

This book is Dedicated to everyone who are a fan of Johnnie Walker and most especially those aspiring to be like him. His relentless pursuit to success consistency and determination.

# TABLE OF CONTENT

# INTRODUCTION

Few radio voices have the ability to immediately arouse feelings, memories, and a connection to a particular era's music. Johnnie Walker has been that voice for decades. He has had lasting impact on the music industry and broadcasting, whether it was through the edgy sounds of pirate radio in the 1960s or the soothing, mellow tones of BBC Radio 2 in the 2000s. However, how did the man behind the microphone come to be adored by generations of listeners, and who is he? The man who would become Johnnie Walker was born Peter Waters Dingley in Birmingham in 1945, and he grew up in a period of social and cultural change. He loved music from a young age and, like many youngsters of his day, was enthralled with the rock and roll explosion. Johnnie's passion for great music extended beyond mere admiration. He got that chance when he joined Radio Caroline, one of the world's most well-known pirate radio stations.

Johnnie got his first taste of what it meant to be a DJ when Radio Caroline, which broadcast from a ship off the coast of England, disregarded the government's ban on pop music. For Johnnie, pirate radio was the ideal venue to launch his career since it was as much about revolt as it was about music. But Johnnie Walker's tale goes beyond his career achievements. It's a very intimate trip filled with highs and lows. Johnnie experienced many difficulties off the air, including severe health issues and drug struggles, despite his amazing success on it. His personal life occasionally threatened to eclipse his job, but Johnnie always managed to bounce back stronger, propelled by his love of radio and music. The main events of Johnnie Walker's life will be covered in this biography, along with how he became a broadcasting pioneer and how he dealt with the evolving radio landscape over the years. This is the tale of a man whose voice influenced the music of millions of lives, starting with his early days as a pirate radio DJ and continuing through his legendary performances on BBC Radio 2, personal struggles, and inspirational comebacks. But beyond the awards, the celebrity, and the well-known voice, Johnnie Walker is a man with an inspirational and accessible tale. He has had difficulties that many of us encounter, whether they be personal or professional, but he has consistently managed to overcome them. His passion for music and audience has always driven him. We will learn about the life of a real radio legend in this book. We'll talk about the man behind the mic, his passion for music, and how he's connected with fans in ways that few others have. It's a tale of tenacity, fervor, and an unshakeable dedication to the broadcasting profession. You'll learn more about Johnnie Walker as a person and a broadcaster as you research him. His tale serves as a reminder that it's never too late to pursue your passion and leave your impact on the world, despite any challenges.

# CHAPTER 1:

## EARLY DAYS AND RADIO BEGINNING

### Growing Up in Birmingham

Jonnie was in Birmingham UK year 1945 with his original birth name **Peter Waters Dingley**, he grew up in a world that was changing quickly. As a young child, Johnnie was inquisitive and vivacious, and the post-war years presented a blend of reconstruction and invention. He grew up surrounded by the sounds of the city, including the buzz of factories, the voices of neighbors, and—above all—the music that seemed to permeate every house. Even in those days, music remained his escape. A young child like Johnnie found the 1950s to be an exciting time. As rock & roll spread across the Atlantic, a new generation of people was being captivated by performers like Chuck Berry, Buddy Holly, and Elvis Presley. Although

Birmingham, England's industrial center, wasn't particularly a center for music, it served as the setting for Johnnie's musical awakening. Early in life, he acquired a passion for records and the radio, and he would frequently stay up late to listen to the newest music on far-off radio stations. Nobody could have predicted how the lad from Birmingham would eventually alter music consumption in the United Kingdom. His love of broadcasting and sharing music with others was sparked by his inquisitive and exploratory childhood.

# First Step into Broadcasting

Without much interrogation, Johnnie made his first broadcasting effort with unwavering conviction. The magic of radio, the close relationship between the DJ and the listener that felt both universal and personal, captivated him, as it did many of his generation. Working at a garage and selling cars in Solihull was how he started, but the desire to be in front of the microphone never went away. Johnnie quickly made his way into local radio, but in a surprising manner. He was hired at a small station, which was his first serious opportunity. Johnnie persisted despite the lack of glamour and the fact that the job was frequently technical rather than artistic. He began to gain confidence in front of the microphone, grasp the subtleties of broadcasting, and learn the ropes. Despite the fact that he was not yet well-known, Johnnie's voice had an indisputable quality. This warm and familiar tone made listeners feel like they were hearing from a friend. He stood out for his love of music and obvious communication skills. Johnnie soon discovered that his aspirations of being on the radio were not only feasible, but also within his reach as the local jobs opened up larger prospects.

## Joining the Radio Caroline: The Pirate Radio Era

The 1960s were a period of musical revolt in addition to political and cultural upheaval. There was a huge void in the market for the kind of rock and roll that young people were craving because of the BBC's conservative stance on pop music, which dominated British radio. Enter pirate radio stations like Radio Caroline, which broadcast from international waters without interference from the government, defying the established quo. And Johnnie Walker would leave his stamp here. Johnnie made the bold decision to join Radio Caroline in 1966, which would come to define his career. Radio Caroline was a beacon of freedom and revolt, broadcasting from a ship off the coast of England. It became the preferred station for young people who were craving the newest rock and pop songs since it aired the music that the

BBC refused to. It was the ideal location for Johnnie. He was one of the station's most popular DJs due to his charm and music passion. Storms, loneliness, and the continual fear of government action to shut them down were all part of ship life, but for Johnnie, it was thrilling. By introducing a generation of listeners to the sounds of The Beatles, The Rolling Stones, and The Who, he contributed to a revolution in broadcasting. His tenure on Radio Caroline was the start of a legacy that would permanently alter British radio, not merely a phase in his career.

# CHAPTER 2:

# THE RISE OF A RADIO STAR

## A Life on Radio Caroline

There was nothing typical about his life in Radio Caroline. The station's mission for Johnnie Walker and his fellow DJs was to push boundaries and create something revolutionary, not just play music. Operating outside of British law and broadcasting from a ship in the North Sea, Radio Caroline allowed its DJs to play the music they loved without any limitations. It was a dream come true for Johnnie. However, life aboard a ship wasn't always as glamorous as it appeared. The DJs had to deal with choppy waves, erratic weather patterns, and the remoteness of being so far from the mainland. However, these difficulties only strengthened the crew's relationship. Radio Caroline was known for its famous camaraderie. A varied and captivating listening experience was produced by the distinct musical tastes and styles that each DJ contributed. In this setting, Johnnie flourished and became one of the station's most adored voices. The identity of the station was significantly shaped by the listeners as well. They were fervently devoted, frequently expressing their love for their favorite DJs in letters or requests that captured the rebellious zeitgeist of the day. These fans responded well to Johnnie's friendly and laid-back demeanor, and he soon rose to prominence as one of the most identifiable voices on the radio. For Johnnie Walker, life on Radio Caroline marked the start of his ascent to radio fame and was more than simply a job.

# Revolutionizing Music on the Airwaves

The music and broadcasting industries themselves were evolving while Johnnie Walker was on Radio Caroline. The BBC dominated UK radio until that point, and their programming was sparse and frequently featured music that catered to an older demographic. There were few ways for young people to listen to the newest songs from bands like The Kinks, The Rolling Stones, and The Beatles. DJs like Johnnie and Radio Caroline intervened to transform the radio landscape at that point.

Other stations would not play the music that Radio Caroline dared to play. Johnnie and his colleagues DJs took satisfaction in introducing their listeners to new bands, obscure songs, and music from beyond the mainstream, so it wasn't just about the huge successes. This change had a significant impact on the future of rock and roll in the UK by providing a platform to musicians who would not have otherwise been able to get airplay.

For Johnnie, creating an experience was more important than simply spinning music. He realized that radio was about more than just playing music; it was about establishing a relationship with listeners and helping them navigate the constantly changing music industry. He was a pioneer in radio because of his ability to capture the passion and feelings of his listeners. By bringing the lively culture of the 1960s straight into people's homes, he was doing more than just playing music; he was also helping to reimagine what radio could be.

# Walkers Influences on 1960s Pop Culture

The impact of Johnnie Walker went much beyond radio. He was playing a significant role in forming the pop culture of the time by the middle of the 1960s. With bands like The Beatles, The Rolling Stones, and The Who at the forefront, the UK was at the epicenter of the musical revolution. Johnnie in particular and Radio Caroline were instrumental in popularizing this song. Johnnie, one of the station's top DJs, came to represent the youth movement, the rebellion, and the zeitgeist.Johnnie evolved into a cultural figure in addition to being a DJ. He was a trusted voice in a world that was changing quickly because of his connection to the music and the listeners. He was living pop culture, not only reporting on it. He was a tastemaker because of his on-air commentary, his conversations with musicians, and his ability to sense the mood of the young people. The music that Johnnie played on Radio Caroline frequently became the background music for young people's lives throughout the United Kingdom. However, Johnnie had an impact on more than simply the music. His own demeanor, disposition, and manner perfectly captured the essence of the 1960s. Everything he did reflected the era's inventiveness, freedom, and resistance. Johnnie Walker left a legacy that touched on the decade's larger cultural movement in addition to music, helping to shape rather than merely reflect contemporary culture.

# CHAPTER 3:

# THE BBC RADIO 1 AND 2 JOURNEY

## Transitioning to BBC Radio 1

After his Wild Range of success in Radio Caroline's, Johnnie Walker's decided to start a new career with BBC Radio 1. The BBC took advantage of the 1967 British government shutdown of pirate radio stations to start a pop music-focused channel. Of course, they desired the same voices that had enthralled youthful listeners all throughout the country. Although it wasn't without difficulties, Johnnie's journey from pirate radio rebel to popular BBC DJ signaled the start of an exciting new chapter in his career.

In 1969, Johnnie brought his distinct approach to BBC Radio 1. He was a tastemaker who was well-known for his genuine love of music, not just another DJ spinning the newest tunes. Compared to his carefree days on Radio Caroline, Radio 1 was different. Even though the show had more official programming, more strict playlists, and more stringent standards, Johnnie was still able to add his own unique touch. He stood out due to his easygoing, conversational attitude and strong bond with his audience.

Instead of dampening his spirit, Johnnie was able to reach a larger audience by moving from the wild world of pirate radio to the more controlled setting of the BBC. His transfer to BBC Radio 1 demonstrated that Johnnie could remain real and continue to influence the music landscape for listeners throughout the United Kingdom, even in a more corporate environment.

# Walkers Breakthrough at BBC 2

Johnnie Walker became one of the most well-known voices in British radio by the late 1970s, but it was his move to BBC Radio 2 that gave him his big break. His career took a significant shift with this move, which allowed him to reach a wider and marginally more sophisticated audience. Radio 2 was renowned for its more varied and eclectic programming, which was ideal for Johnnie's wide-ranging tastes, whereas Radio 1 catered to the youth.Johnnie discovered a place where he could really excel at BBC Radio 2. He created playlists that combined the greatest pop, rock, and other iconic sounds, putting his years of experience and extensive musical knowledge front and center. His voice, which millions of people now recognize, became a reassuring sound on the radio. In addition to the music, Johnnie's friendly and gregarious demeanor drew listeners in. He had a remarkable talent for making every performance feel intimate, as though he were addressing each audience member individually. Johnnie's success at Radio 2 was more about developing as a presenter than it was about attracting more listeners. He bridged the gap between the revolutionary sounds of the 1960s and the shifting musical environment of the 1970s and 1980s, becoming a voice of continuity for generations of music enthusiasts. His reputation as a radio icon was cemented by his success at BBC Radio 2.

## The Sound of the 70s Defining an Era

Because of his renowned show, The Sound of the 70s, Johnnie Walker became a symbol of the music and culture of the 1970s. For music, the 1970s were a pivotal decade. As rock & roll changed, new subgenres like disco, punk, and glam rock appeared, each adding a distinct taste to the radio. For music fans, Johnnie's show is a must-listen because of his ability to adjust and stay ahead of these trends. The goal of The Sound of the Seventies was to capture the spirit of a generation, not just play the newest songs. By combining chart-topping songs with deeper cuts and providing airtime to up-and-coming artists who would later define the decade, Johnnie's show mirrored the diversity of the era. His performance included lesser-known performers that Johnnie supported in addition to well-known performers like David Bowie, Elton John, and Queen. His audience trusted him because he didn't hesitate to take chances. Beyond just music, Johnnie was able to establish the decade's sound. His presence and voice became ingrained in the culture of the 1970s. The Sound of the Seventies served as the background music for daily living, whether you were driving, lounging around the house, or spending time with friends. Many people will always associate that time period with Johnnie Walker's voice because he not only performed the song but also lived it.

# CHAPTER 4:

# PERSONAL STRUGGLES AND COMBACKS

## Battling Personal Demons Health and Addiction

Johnnie Walker was battling personal issues behind the polished voice and amiable demeanor his fans adored. His work and celebrity pressures began to affect his health, as they do for many celebrities. As he was enjoying his popularity in the 1970s, Johnnie began to battle addiction, a problem that would influence the next stage of his life. Although discussing addiction is never simple, Johnnie found that the only way to take back control of his life was to confront it head-on. His drug and alcohol addiction hampered his judgment throughout this trying time and impacted his relationships, both personal and professional. Few people were aware of the emotional struggle he was going through at the height of his success. Despite the protracted and agonizing struggle with these inner demons, Johnnie was adamant on finding a solution. The fact that he decided to face these problems instead of allowing them to define him is evidence of his fortitude and tenacity. Even though it wasn't an effortless journey, Johnnie's choice to get help signaled the start of a life-changing event. His candidness about his difficulties later served as motivation for many, demonstrating that there is hope even in the direst circumstances. This phase of his life was about discovering a new sense of purpose rather than merely surviving.

## Leaving Radio for a Fresh Start

After so many years of having this personal struggles, Walker decided to risk all in the early 1980s by leaving radio. This wasn't an effortless decision for a man whose voice has been a constant in so many people's lives. For Johnnie, however, it was essential. He realized that in order to recover from the damage caused by his struggle with addiction, he needed to start over, away from the demands of his job. Leaving radio meant more than simply quitting a profession; it was venturing into the unknown. Johnnie had to discover his identity without the microphone for the first time in decades. His life during this time was characterized by introspection and introspection. He focused on restoring his physical, mental, and emotional well-being while traveling and spending time with loved ones. Even though it was a tough choice, it gave him the opportunity to re-establish a connection with himself that had been unattainable while he was enmeshed in the chaos of his profession. Johnnie was also able to gain a fresh perspective on his life and business during this time away. It was a much-needed break rather than the end of his quest. Sometimes stepping back is the only way to go forward, and Johnnie found that leaving radio gave him the fortitude and clarity he needed to eventually return. His leaving was an opportunity to start afresh, not a farewell.

# A Remarkable Moment His Return to Airwaves

After years of introspection and personal hardship, Johnnie Walker was prepared to triumphantly return to the radio by the mid-1980s. Regaining his passion and demonstrating to his audience and himself that he still had a lot more to contribute were the main goals of his comeback, not only going back to work. It felt like a new beginning when he returned to radio, bringing with him not just his extensive musical knowledge but also a renewed feeling of humility and wisdom. It was like welcoming an old friend back into the fold when Johnnie rejoined BBC Radio. His return delighted listeners who had grown up with his voice, but he also added a sense of honesty and tenacity that further enhanced his appeal. It was evident that Johnnie had become stronger as a result of the struggles he had endured, and his voice reflected the weight of his experiences.

Additionally, Johnnie's return symbolized something greater—a message of rebirth and optimism. He had conquered his demons, stepped away from the spotlight, and come back not only as the beloved DJ but also as a person who had gracefully surmounted his obstacles. His homecoming was one of the most touching moments in his career because of the way his story of tenacity and recovery struck a chord with the audience. Johnnie Walker's return to radio marked the beginning of a new chapter in his life, one that was full of fortitude, direction, and a strong bond with his listeners.

# CHAPTER 5:

# LEGENDARY SHOWS AND MEMORABLE MOMENTS

## The Radio 2 Drivetime Show

The Radio 2 Drivetime Show, one of Johnnie Walker's most famous programs, swiftly gained popularity among listeners on their daily commute. The Drivetime show, which debuted in the late 1990s, served as a companion for those dealing with the strains of everyday life in addition to being a means of filling the airways during rush hour. Listeners came in for Johnnie's calming voice, expertly chosen music, and captivating commentary, whether they were stuck in traffic or settling down after a long day. Combining his passion for music with his innate ability to connect with people, Johnnie turned the Drivetime show into something truly unique. In addition to simply performing songs, he was sharing memories, narrating stories, and giving each song a unique vibe. Despite being on a crowded highway, his relaxed yet polished manner gave listeners the impression that they were having a private conversation with him. However, the show's legendary status was not just due to its music. Every program was made more friendly and humorous by Johnnie, who frequently included entertaining segments and interactive elements to keep viewers interested. For fans of all ages, Johnnie made Drivetime a must-listen, whether he was introducing a new artist, performing a classic, or sharing a story from his decades in the business. One of the highlights of his lengthy and illustrious career, the show became a mainstay of BBC Radio 2.

# Interviews with Icons; Guest and Conversations

Johnnie Walker had the chance to interview some of the biggest personalities in music over his career, and his performances featured these interviews as iconic moments. Johnnie stands out as a broadcaster because he can get to the heart of any talk, whether it's with pop icons, rock stars, or up-and-coming artists. He treated each guest with genuine curiosity and respect, fostering an environment where they felt at ease sharing their story rather than using an aggressive or confrontational interview technique. Johnnie's interview with the legendary Beatles George Harrison stands out as one of his most remarkable interviews. The conversation covered a wide range of topics, including spirituality, personal development, and the evolving nature of celebrity, in addition to music. Listeners were given a unique look into the private life of one of the biggest stars in the world, and Johnnie's bond with Harrison was evident. Johnnie also conducted interviews with other musical icons over the years, including Elton John, Paul McCartney, and David Bowie. Every discussion was different, full of wit, humor, and unguarded moments. Not because of any shocking disclosures, but rather because of the way Johnnie let his guests be themselves, these interviews became a mainstay of his presentations. The purpose of Johnnie's interviews was to capture the spirit of the musician behind the songs, not merely to promote new albums or concerts.

# The Gold Stranded Honoring Musical Legends

It was always clear that Johnnie Walker loved and respected music, but it was especially clear when he paid tribute to musical greats during his concerts. He was more than just a DJ spinning the songs; he was an ardent supporter of the musicians who influenced the music of whole generations. Johnnie made it a point to honor the musical traditions of the artists who had made a lasting impression on the business through his numerous radio shows. Johnnie accomplished this, among other things, by committing special portions to legendary musicians, frequently on the anniversaries of their albums or at pivotal points in their careers. These tributes were thoughtfully constructed tours of an artist's life and influence rather than merely compilations of songs. Listeners gained a greater understanding of the music they liked as a result of Johnnie's sharing of rare tunes, personal tales, and observations. Johnnie established the benchmark for paying homage to musical icons, whether it was by paying homage to Elvis Presley, delving deeply into The Rolling Stones' discography, or commemorating Queen's lasting legacy. However, it went beyond the past. Johnnie also had a knack for spotting future stars and frequently supported up-and-coming musicians before they were well known. He was a respected voice in the music industry because of his ability to strike a balance between nostalgia and fresh sounds. Honoring musical legends was more than just a part of Johnnie Walker's work; it was a personal goal to make sure that these musicians' talents would never be forgotten.

# CHAPTER 6:

# WALKERS IMPACT IN MUSIC AND BROADCASTING

## Championing New Artist

Johnnie Walker has consistently demonstrated a talent for seeing potential before it became popular throughout his career. He stands out from other broadcasters due to his sincere love of music and acute sense of distinctive sounds. Johnnie took satisfaction in providing exposure to emerging artists who were still establishing themselves in the industry, when many other DJs concentrated on well-known performers. This ability to identify up-and-coming talent became a hallmark of his performances in the early years of his career. He brought his fans new, daring songs by not being scared to stray from the tried-and-true options and venture into the unknown. This strategy influenced the tone of British radio in addition to helping innumerable performers become well-known. Johnnie offered a platform that could launch careers, from promoting up-and-coming artists to releasing songs by future legends like David Bowie. Being included on Johnnie Walker's show was a major accomplishment for a lot of performers. It indicated that someone who genuinely understood the music business and saw your potential had noticed you. In order to ensure that the upcoming generation of musicians could leave their imprint, Johnnie took the role of finding new performers very seriously.

# The Role of DJs in Shaping UK Music Scene

The UK music scene was greatly influenced by DJs like Johnnie Walker, particularly in the 1960s and 1970s, when radio was the main medium for discovering new music. However, Johnnie's impact extended beyond his record-spinning abilities. He belonged to a new generation of DJs who could define what "cool," affect musical preferences was, and even influence cultural trends. Johnnie developed as a tastemaker while working at Radio Caroline and then BBC Radio 1 and 2. His playlist was determined by his sincere passion for music rather than by record labels or marketing departments. Because of his genuineness, he was able to expose viewers to genres that they might not have otherwise investigated. Johnnie performed music that challenged conventions and sparked conversations, whether it was rock, pop, or the new sounds of punk. In addition to the music,

Johnnie's on-air presence contributed to a redefining of the DJ's job. He was more than simply a voice on the microphone; he was a person who the audience could relate to and trusted. Because of the strong bond between the audience and the DJ, DJs like Johnnie were able to inspire movements in addition to playing music. Johnnie Walker was at the vanguard of the evolution of the UK music scene, which was shaped not only by the musicians but also by the DJs who shared their sounds with the general public.

## Awards, Recognitions and Legacy

Not everyone has heard of Johnnie Walker's contributions to music and broadcasting and looked away. His many honors and recognitions over the years attest to the enduring influence of his contributions. These distinctions, which range from fan appreciation to industry honors, bear witness to his influence on the careers and broadcasts of innumerable musicians. His admission into the Radio Academy Hall of Fame was one of his most notable accomplishments. His decades-long career and his impact on the development of British radio were acknowledged with this distinction. Johnnie has also won praise for his efforts in music promotion, his interviews with music icons, and his exceptional capacity to establish a personal connection with listeners. However, Johnnie's legacy is something much more lasting than the tangible honors. By fusing his passion for music with a profound regard for the art of broadcasting, he has made a lasting impression on the cultural landscape of the United Kingdom. Millions of people's lives were made better by his voice, and his impact will continue to motivate broadcasters in the future. Building ties with his fans, the musicians he supported, and the music he enjoys has always been Johnnie's real reward. His impact on people's lives and the music he has shared are more significant than his accolades.

# CHAPTER 7:

# HIS LIFE BEYOND MICROPHONE

## Personal Life Family and Passion

Even though Johnnie Walker is most recognized for his distinctive radio voice, his personal life is an integral and significant aspect of his identity. Family and personal interests have always been essential to Johnnie outside of the studio. His life revolves around his relationship with his wife, Tiggy. They have experienced the highs and lows of his profession together, encouraging one another at challenging times and sharing in their victories. Their relationship, which has endured through all of life's hardships, is proof of the value of love and cooperation. In addition to his family, Johnnie enjoys a variety of pastimes. Classic vehicles are one of his greatest passions. He frequently works on or drives old cars in his spare time because he finds them fascinating. He can engage in a lifelong interest and find a welcome respite from the hectic world of broadcasting through this activity. also, Johnnie has a strong spiritual connection. His life's path has led him to investigate inner peace, mindfulness, and meditation, all of which have assisted him in navigating the highs and lows of his personal and professional lives. His larger-than-life presence that many people are familiar with from the radio has been balanced by his family, passions, and spiritual practices.

## Philanthropy and Charity work

Johnnie Walker has devoted a significant amount of his time and efforts to charitable work and philanthropy throughout the years. He is passionate about supporting initiatives that assist people suffering similar circumstances because of his life experiences, which include his struggles with addiction and health issues. Action on Addiction, a charity that helps individuals overcome drug and alcohol addiction, is one of the causes he cares about the most. Johnnie's candor about his own experience has encouraged others to get treatment and helped dispel the stigma associated with addiction. Johnnie has been active in many other charity projects in addition to his involvement with addiction recovery. He has donated to mental health awareness campaigns, backed cancer research groups, and assisted in raising money for causes ranging from animal welfare to homelessness. Throughout his life, he has shown compassion and a desire to change the world for the better. Johnnie has always supported using his position to spread the word about worthy causes. He has continuously used his platform to assist others, whether it be by hosting charity broadcasts, organizing fundraising events, or just speaking up for people in need. His charitable endeavors demonstrate his faith in generosity, camaraderie, and the value of giving back.

# The Future Continue to Inspire the Future Generations

Despite decades of broadcasting success, Johnnie Walker remains passionate and optimistic about the future. Even though he is now considered a legend, his quest is far from finished. Johnnie's talent and commitment are demonstrated by his ability to adjust and remain relevant in a media industry that is constantly evolving. Johnnie continues to be an important voice in the industry, whether it be through his new endeavors or his ongoing appearance on BBC Radio 2.

Johnnie's influence on upcoming generations of music fans and broadcasters is among his greatest legacies. His sincere passion for radio and his unafraid stance in supporting up-and-coming artists have had a profound impact on the business. Young DJs and presenters frequently credit him as a major influence on their careers because they respect his genuineness, love of telling stories, and capacity to establish a personal connection with listeners.

Johnnie is dedicated to carrying on with his broadcasting career in the future while simultaneously coaching and supporting the upcoming generation of talent. For him, radio is a craft that should be fostered and maintained, not merely a job. Johnnie sees countless opportunities in the future, and he will continue to be a cherished and significant person in the radio industry as long as there are tales to tell, songs to share, and lives to impact.

# CONCLUSION

As we get to the end of Johnnie Walker's incredible journey, it is evident that his life is a tribute to the strength of ardor, fortitude, and genuineness. From his modest upbringing in Birmingham to his rise to fame in the broadcasting industry, Johnnie's tale is not only one of career achievement; it is also one of personal adversity, victory, and a strong dedication to the craft of music and storytelling.

In addition to entertaining millions of people during his storied career, Johnnie has served as an inspiration to innumerable musicians and budding broadcasters. His bold attitude to music, especially his steadfast encouragement of up-and-coming artists, has had a significant impact on the UK music landscape. He has shown that a DJ's job description goes well beyond the microphone and includes the ability to inspire, motivate, and establish a human connection with his audience.

Johnnie's path is also characterized by his dedication to generosity, demonstrating that genuine legacy is determined by one's beneficial influence on others rather than only by awards. He is a relatable character who demonstrates that it's acceptable to struggle and ask for assistance because of his work with charity and his candor about personal struggles. Many people have been moved by this vulnerability, which has inspired others to bravely and honestly accept their own experiences.

Johnnie Walker continues to be a source of inspiration for the future. His commitment to developing fresh talent and a passion for music guarantees that his impact will last for many decades. He personifies the essence of radio, a medium that unites people via common experiences and tales, even in the face of shifting entertainment and technological trends.

When we consider Johnnie Walker's life and work, we are reminded that greatness is characterized by the relationships we create, the lives we impact, and the happiness we spread rather than just by success or notoriety. We honor not only a radio legend but also a real defender of music, kindness, and the human spirit as his voice reverberates across the airways. Cheers to Johnnie Walker, a legend whose tale continues to inspire us all and whose journey is far from over.

Printed in Great Britain
by Amazon

49776757R00031